Cranmer and Pole — Archbishops

Acknowledgements
Some of these poems were previously published in the *Cranmer* chapbook (Broken Jaw Press, ISBN 0-921411-66-9, 1997) and read by the author on *Impressions* (TVNB/Shaw).

Cover illustrations by Todd Hawkes and Joe Blades after the painting "Thomas Cranmer, Archbishop and Martyr" by Gerhard Fliche (1546) in the National Portrait Gallery, England, and an unattributed image of Pole from Westminster Cathedral Library, England.
Author photo by Todd Hawkes.
Design and in-house editing by Joe Blades.
Printed and bound in Canada.

This book is also published by eBooks (ISBN 1-896647-40-5) in PDF format with distribution by PublishingOnline.Com

The Publisher acknowledges the support of the Canada Council for the Arts and New Brunswick's Arts Development Branch for our publishing program.

Broken Jaw Press
Box 596 Stn A
Fredericton NB E3B 5A6
Canada
www.brokenjaw.com
tel / fax 506 454-5127
jblades@nbnet.nb.ca

Canadian Cataloguing in Publication Data
Hawkes, Robert, 1930-

Cranmer and Pole

Poems.
ISBN 1-896647-33-2

1. Cranmer, Thomas, 1489-1556 — Poetry. 2. Pole, Reginald, 1500-1558 — poetry. I. Title.

PS8565.A84C732 2000 C811'.54 C99-950093-6
PR9199-3.H365C732 2000

Cranmer and Pole Archbishops

Robert Hawkes

Fredericton • Canada

In memory of my Grandmother
Bertha Irene (Cox) Hawkes

and

for Lorraine, Marissa, Madison and Mallory
for whom the Old Faith will be forever new

Foreword

Based on the research materials available to me, I have attempted to see into the heart and mind of both Archbishop Cranmer and Reginald Cardinal Pole. *Cranmer and Pole — Archbishops* is my creation of what I perceive the essence of each man to be.

While preparing to write about Cranmer, whom I had wanted to honour for his role in creating the *Book of Common Prayer*, I kept coming upon references to Pole, Cranmer's successor as Archbishop of Canterbury. It was the human drama of his life story that led me to attempt a portrayal of him.

More has been written about Thomas Cranmer than about Cardinal Pole. I therefore had to invent several occasions to present the Cardinal's views as I understood them. In attempting to portray Cranmer, however, the task was somewhat different. Given the number of biographies about the man, I was required to choose between versions of events that were sometimes at variance. The versions I chose naturally corresponded with the Thomas Cranmer who took up residence in my head.

I would like to thank my wife Peggy Hawkes and my friend and former colleague George Haley for their advice and criticism in my writing this work. I would also like to thank Joe Blades, owner and publisher of Broken Jaw Press, for having the courage to publish both *Cranmer*, as a chapbook, and *Cranmer and Pole — Archbishops*.

Robert Hawkes
Fredericton, NB
Spring 2000

Cranmer

Excerpts from a letter he might have written to his friend Alexander Aless in the early morning hours of March 21, 1556

Blessed lord, which hast caused all holy Scriptures to bee written for our learning; graunte us that we may in suche wise heare them, read, marke, learne, and inwardly digeste them; that by pacience, and coumfort of thy holy worde, we may embrace, and euer holde fast the blessed hope of everlasting life, which thou hast geuen us in our sauiour Jesus Christe.

— The Collect for the Second Sunday in Advent
from the *First Prayer-Book of Edward VI*, 1549

1.

It took me
seven weeks
to return
from Mantua
after I learned
Henry had
nominated me
to be archbishop

The December roads
of France were
icier than usual
that year
but reluctance
was the cause
of my delay
for I knew
if I accepted
I would have
to traverse
the Great Matter
of the King
forever

2

I accepted
the primacy
though I knew
a bishop's staff
could easily
turn into
a stake

I was willing
to run this risk
in order to serve
both my Lord God
and my Sovereign

3

Eight years ago
I was called
to Henry's bedside

He lay dying
and voiceless
but he grasped
my right hand
and held onto it
until the end

That same hand
I shall thrust
into the flames
at once

It must be
punished first
for having written
the recantations
I shall renounce
when I speak
before my burning

4

The 11 heretics
I helped play
a part in sending
to the stake
have filed past me
for a fortnight
with their arms
outstretched

It may be
that in death
they know
I took no pleasure
in condemning them
and did not go
to watch them
turn to ash

At the head
of the column
is young Firth
the Cantabrigian
who refused
the opportunity
the guards gave him
to escape
in Brixton Wood
on his way
from the Tower
to my Palace

I must admit,
dear friend,
I admired him
and the other 10
for holding onto
their beliefs
however silly
or unorthodox
they were

5

Do you recall
the beetle trapped
on the cedar log
whose burning
warmed our bones
five years ago

It crawled
back and forth
back and forth
as it tried
to escape

Then suddenly
it rushed
headlong
into the flames

After Cole has said
what he has to say
and I have said
what I have to say
like that beetle
I shall rush
through the rain
to the stake
and never once
look back

6

Just two nights
of dreams ago
I woke up
sweat-drenched
from watching
two kings
jousting for
my soul

One with the voice
of Henry raged
I was his creature
while he tried
to unhorse
King Jesus
who replied:

You are wrong
for he is mine
forever

7

I was the last
of the Council
to sign the devise
naming Lady Jane
as the next monarch

and I only did so
because Edward
as my Sovereign
asked me to

I told Mary this
in a letter
she will not read

I also told her
that consonant
with God's laws
I am willing
to serve her
in any way
she asks
because she is
my Sovereign

I also said
I would accept
the Pope as head
of the English church
if that was
as Sovereign
her wish

Yet I was
found guilty
on a charge
of treason
and sentenced
to dismemberment
on Tyburn Hill
before my enemies
and a circus —
seeking rabble

8

Lying sleepless
in Bocardo gaol
I sometimes ask
myself

How did Columbus feel
far out on the ocean
seeking a westward passage
to the Middle Land

Did he look homeward
often saying to himself:

Maybe I should go back
to the continent I know
rather than to try to go
where no one else has

9

I am most proud
of having helped
create the Book
of Common Prayer

I believe
it contains
the essentials
for salvation

and does so
in a language
God would be
proud to speak

10

I think
of metaphors
as explorers
into worlds
no one has
travelled in
before

But I also see
how easily
such journies
may lead
the seeker
into danger

11

As Thomas Cantuar
I strove in vain
to bring together
in one house

all who profess
that Jesus Christ
is verily the Son
of Our Father God

But each builder had
his own blueprint
and would not work
from any other

As you can imagine
the foundation was
not congruent with
the sills hewn for it

Nor did the doors
and windows fit
the frames set
in place for them

12

The agreeing
to a divorce
between Anne
and Henry
is the one act
of which I am
most ashamed

He did not
want to have
a Queen
beheaded
so in Convocation
we decided
there were
grounds for
a divorce

The grounds
for which
I doubt
will ever
be made known

13

When I learned
Anne was accused
of sexual misconduct

I wrote
these words
to Henry:

> Your Grace best knoweth
> that next unto Your Grace
> I am most bound unto her
> of all creatures living

I was later
informed
I had
put my life
in danger
for telling Henry
how I felt

But Anne had
been my friend
as had her family
since I first came
to London

14

On the night
before she died
when she had
nothing left
to lose
Anne insisted
she was innocent
of all charges

You will recall
finding me
walking up
and down
the paths
of Lambeth
at 4 a.m.
after my return
from hearing
her confession

It is true
I did kiss
my brother
on the lips

she said

but he was
not my lover

I was just
so happy
to see someone
who was not
a vulture
circling
around me
as Henry
for reasons
I do not know
withdrew his love
and listened to
my enemies

both at home
and across
the Channel

If only I
had given him
a son

15

Some of my accusers
say I was a sandbar
shifting location
at every Henry whim

I prefer to say
I was a navigator
struggling to steer
the English church

through the Scylla
of Henry's morning
and the Charybdis
of his afternoon

With young Edward
the seas were calmer
but with Mary
the ship is foundering

When I pleaded
with her father
not to send her
to the Tower

he acceded
saying I would
one day regret
what I was asking

16

Other accusers say
I was putty
in the hands
of Henry

I disagree
but I would say
at times
he could be
dried putty
when he had
made up his mind

I often tried
to get him
to change
his mind

These attempts
my accusers do
not know about
for they were
made in private

17

At my trial
for heresy
I was charged
with being
an adulterer
because I had
taken a wife

My response:
Better to marry
than take
a concubine

18

I supported Henry
when he decreed
that priests
who marry
should be
put to death

However I sent
Margaret with
our children
to the Germanies
where they are now
once again
for fear
Mary order
their arrest

19

One of the many
many falsehoods
making the rounds
about me is that
I took my wife
with me from place
to place hidden
in a padded tun
into which holes
had been drilled
for her to breathe
through

20

Since withholding
such knowledge was
an act of treason
those in the know
begged me to convey
to Henry their belief
that his fourth queen
was taking other men
into her bed

I did not have the heart
to say the words to him
so with trembling hands
while we were in church
I handed him a note
that he might be informed
about the matter

21

I do not believe
that bread and wine
become the very flesh
and blood of Christ

Whatever change
there is is in
the hearts of those
who eat and drink

I wish to point out
that in these beliefs
I simply reaffirm
the early Fathers

22

I cannot deny
that until today
I have for a month
turned my back
on everything
I held as true

I have sat
many hours
in this cell
asking why

trying to find
an answer
that will bring
me peace
before they slip
an iron cage
around my chest
to hold my body
to the stake

  Did I recant
  (as Mary says)
  to save myself
  from the flames

  Did I hope
  to outlive her
  and continue
  my reforms

I do know
that something
in me snapped
when the gaoler
refused even
to say hello

Robert Hawkes

For two years
he had been
my only friend
in Bocardo gaol

and often prayed
with and for me
that I might see
the light
of the Old Faith

23.

Who should preside
at my degrading
but Bishop Bonner
whom I sometimes
had to reprimand
during my primacy

He was assisted
by Bishop Thirlby
who I thought
was my friend

And maybe so
for he wept
as he scraped
my fingertips
to punish them
for having
falsely carried
out the functions
of archbishop

Bonner smiled
as he scraped
and scraped
my offending
digits

24

God knows
there is little
to laugh at
these days

but I smile
at the metaphor
of myself
as an onion
at my degrading

Wearing as heart
this tattered shirt
I was commanded
to put on the garb
of all the orders
from the lowest
in ascending order
to the pall
of an archbishop
which served
as the onionskin

Then I was told
to peel off
one by one
all the layers
of my ecclesial clothes
until I stood
completely peeled
before the mob
clad in the shirt
I referred to
as the heart

But my metaphor does
not hold for my mitre
which was yanked
off my head
and replaced
with a greasy
and illfitting
ratcatcher's hat
after a barber had
shaved the hair
off my head

25

I am grateful
they did not
touch my beard
at my degrading
for I have
let it grow
since the day
of Henry's death
as witness
to my grief

26

Did I recant
because I had
doubts about
my reading
as metaphor
what Jesus may
have thought of
as simple fact
about the bread
and wine

27

For the past two years
much younger priests than I
have tried to show me
where I erred
after my study
of the Holy Bible
the early Fathers
such as Augustine
and the Scholastics
for example
Peter Lombard
and the great Aquinas

Not only do
they lecture me
but they pray
that I will climb
out of the sty
I have been
wallowing in
for decades

28

For seven hours
I stood alone
debating 33 divines
on the nature
of the Eucharist
while those
looking on
brimful
of ale
jeered at
my remarks
and clapped
their hands
at everything
my opponents
said

29

Those in charge
of my burning
have asked me
to recite
the Ave Maria
at the end
of my remarks

They will be
most surprised
to hear me say
that I renounce
my recantation
and reaffirm all
that I believe
to be true

I only pray that
for those who have
believed in me
it is not too little
and too late

30

In Babylonia
an eye for an eye
was sufficient

In England
a life for a life
does not suffice
for it seems
my death will
not avenge that
of Bishop Fisher
whom I beseeched
Henry to allow
to swear to the Oath
of Succession
minus the preamble
thereby keeping him
off the scaffold

31

A heavy rain is
now falling
over Oxford

I pray it will
not dampen
the faggots
piled up
around me

More loudly
than ever
I hear the screams
of Bishop Ridley
while the wood
sputtered
and smouldered
around him
hour after hour

Since they refused
to tie a gunpowder belt
around his waist
I have no hope
they will ease me
into death

32

The clock has
just struck five
and my flesh still
gives shelter
to my soul

Soon though
it will be
a handful
of ashes
in the ditch
running along
the north wall
of Oxford

I am hopeful
my soul will
find a home
in heaven

33

Dear friend,
do not mistake
what I write
as self-pity

Like all men
I die a sinner
but I have
great hope
God will
stretch out
his arms
to me

May angels protect you
until you too stand
at heaven's gate

Pole

The Cardinal Archbishop

{M}y commission is of grace and clemency
to such as will receive it.
For touching all matters that be past,
they shall be as things cast into the sea
of forgetfulness.

—Reginald Cardinal Pole
at Whitehall on November 28, 1554

April 20, 1520**

My tutors enunciate
this principle:

One must walk
into the past
before walking
into the future

Therefore they insist
I learn not only Latin
but Greek as well
for they believe
the latter is
the pathway
to the wisdom
of the Ancient Greeks
and the Early Fathers

December 30, 1521*

At Oxford I learned
classical Greek
with Latimer
and Linacre

And now at Padua
I am reading Plato
with Nicolo Tomeo
as my guide

He is a scholar
of the Classics
without peer
in the entire world

I am most grateful
to my cousin Henry
for sending me here

I do wonder though
if all the people who dine
at my table do so
because I am known
as the kinsman
of the English king

December 25, 1528**

Why are you weeping
on the morning
of Christ's birth

I asked my mother
after Mass

Though I stand
before the cradle
of the Christ Child

she replied

three coffins occupy
my memory:

My father's is
the first one

He was attainted
and put to death
in the Tower
when I was seven

My brother's is
the second

The seventh Henry
beheaded him in 1499

Your father's coffin is
the third

You were only five
when he died
so you may have
faint memories
of him

He was much
too young to die
though his was
a natural death

He was after all
only married to
a Plantagenet

May 27, 1529**

Pool by pool
the stream advanced
across the meadow

I peered into each one
expecting to find
a monk at prayer
or a scholar
reading Plato

Nearing the hilltop
I heard the anger
in the water's voice
as it confronted
the quire of boulders
strewn across its path

Wading through
the clover
once again

I asked myself
if one of these
was a metaphor
for my future

December 12, 1530

Yesterday
Cardinal Wolsey died
on his way to the Tower

Had he been able
to prevent the troops
of Catherine's nephew
from pillaging Rome

he might have been able
to persuade Clement
to annul the marriage
of our King and Queen

But he could not
and so he earned
the enmity of Anne
before which his power melted
as if a block of ice
in high summer heat

I have been told
Henry will offer me
the York archbishopric
now that it is vacant

Though he will be
very angry

I shall say no
if he does

August 8, 1535*

People ask:

When threatened
with the axe

why did More and Fisher
not accept Henry
as head of the English Church

I reply:

Under stress
the tongue will not betray
what the heart knows
to be true

I speak from experience

While listening
to Paris *clerici* affirm
Julius did not have the right
to say Henry could marry
his brother's widow

my heart told me
they were wrong

On my return to London
I at first avoided Henry
for I was afraid
to tell him how I felt

However I met him
without warning
in a palace alcove
late one afternoon

and without hesitation
my tongue spoke
for my heart:

Sovereign and cousin,
you must not set
your wife aside

December 22, 1536*

When Henry sent
More and Fisher
to the block

I asked myself
if he was going mad

My answer lay
in the promise he made
to send Fisher's head
off to Rome
for a hat sizing

Since one cannot predict
what madmen will do

it is more likely
twisted logic will decide
my family's fate
than anything I do

Therefore
I have today
put on the biretta
and the sapphire ring

Though I shall never
approach the saintliness
of the martyred Fisher

I shall wear my hat
as though it were his
also

On a happier note:

Paul has heeded
my advice and that
of several others
not to withdraw
his offer of a red hat
to Caraffa

January 28, 1536*

Catherine died
two weeks ago

Sadness was the *alpha*
and *omega* to her life
in England

Her first husband
the Prince of Wales
died shortly after
they were married

And after 22 years
her second marriage
ended in a divorce
she did not acknowledge
and a separation
she did not desire

And as she lay dying
Henry would not allow
Mary to go to her

June 22, 1536*

Catherine and Anne were
once as sweet milk
to Henry

But when they failed
to bear a healthy son

they became as sour milk
to him

So he spat them out
leaving Catherine
without a crown
and Anne Boleyn
without a head

People say
Henry's dancing
with his next queen
the night before
Anne lost her head
is proof he has no heart

Although I agree
it was a tasteless act

I believe he was trying
to outdance his guilt

July 23, 1536*

Erasmus died
11 days ago
in Basel

Those who believe
he helped prepare
the way for Luther
may not share
my sadness

A sadness not eased
with the knowledge
he will be remembered
until the end of time

I believe his mission was
to persuade those doctors
who prefer to argue
rather than to heal
that they should
examine once again
the medicine of Jesus
even if it required them
to learn the language
He wrote his prescription
in

March 23, 1537*

Henry has hired an assassin
or so I have been warned

Whether it will be
a blow on the back
of the head
I do not know

Nor do I know
if he is someone
I think of as a friend

What I do know is
I cannot live in fear
forever

June 24, 1538**

Strolling in my olive grove
this morning

I came upon a dove
lying in the grass

It must have flown
into the wall of glass
on the west side
of my study

Fretful doves formed
a quincunx around
their fallen comrade
and would not let me
near

Within half an hour
it was able to wobble
into the sky

As I watched it
out of sight

I thought of
my eight comrades
as a phalanx
Paul mustered
to protect the Church

The *Consilium*
our defence
of what we pray
will forever be
the spiritual home
of all human beings

September 11, 1538

Thirteen days ago
my brother Geoffrey was
taken to the Tower
where under torture
he repeated conversations
Henry twisted into a plot
to overthrow his dynasty

At once
our brother Henry
and cousin Essex
were arrested
and beheaded
for high treason
and our mother
and little nephew
taken to the Tower

I may have
tipped the scales
against them
by accusing the King
of wild beast behaviour

Can one describe
how he is behaving
in any other way

I believe though
it is the fact
we are Plantagenets
that lies at the root
of Henry's wish
to ruin us

I am told
Geoffrey wanders
around London
as if he were
sleep-walking

Do I sleep so ill
because I am trying
to go in my dreams
to comfort him

September 19, 1538**

The dream recurs every night
like a waterwheel

I have a high fever
caused by a poison
suspected of being
genus Plantagenet

In despair
I ask a surgeon
if he can make me
well again

I certainly can

Henry's voice assures
as I wake up

All I need do is
remove your head

May 27, 1539**

The rain stopped
so I took my guests
onto the terrace
for liqueurs

Ever the poet
Vittoria asked
of the clouds
filling up the sky:

Don't they remind you
of gambolling sheep

Responding first
Ghiberti said
they looked to him
like a garden of roses

Caraffa objected
saying he saw
a flotilla of triremes

Not to be outdone
I suggested a flock
of creamy swans

After 10 minutes
of defending
our metaphors

Caraffa asked:

If these clouds were
the *Holy Scriptures*
would not the people
be confused

June 27, 1541

Two weeks ago
you became a martyr
and I am proud
to be your son

Henry can do
nothing more to you
and at this hour
that does give me
consolation

Had you not been able
to forgive those
who mistreated you

hate would long ago
have burst your heart

I expect
you even forgave
our cousin Henry
for ordering his men
not to give you
one warm blanket
or enough to eat

I can almost imagine
your trying from the grave
to tell the axeman
you forgive him
for having to
smite your neck
so many times

O my mother
My brother
My nephew
My cousin

Dead
All dead

All put to death
by Henry Tudor
whom I once revered

September 13, 1541

Tomorrow I enter
the Patrimonium Petri
as its governor
on behalf of Paul

Knowing I would be
called upon to sign
death warrants

I very nearly did not
accept the office

But Paul agreed
that I should send
to their death
only those who were
beyond redemption

God, I beg you
to hasten the day
that rulers do not
believe they are
cleansing the world
when they kill those
they look upon
with suspicion

August 23, 1542

Jesus set the example
of walking on paths
no one else had trod
and so did Contarini

Many felt he should not
meet the Protestants
at Regensburg

But Paul did
and so did I

So off to Bavaria
the Cardinal went
asking hope and goodwill
to travel with him

After the delegates had
agreed upon a protocol
about the role of faith

their talks broke down
and with a grieving heart
he recrossed the Alps
and never was the same
again

Farewell, dear friend

Though the absence
of your candle takes
from our world its light

I know it is shining
even now in heaven

Farewell again,
my dear dear friend

Your leaving us
has palsied my hand
and I can write no more
tonight

February 22, 1545*

I am honoured
and humbled at
Paul's asking me
to be one of a trio
of cardinals to
preside at Trent

May we there
effect reforms
within the Church
and restore
its unity

The Emperor has asked
that we not discuss
doctrinal matters
until the other side
arrives

I shall endeavour
to honour his request

At the opening
of the Council
I also intend to ask
each of the Fathers
to confess openly
his own sinfulness

And so shall I
for I believe
to do so is the first step
toward the liberation
Christ's atonement
offers

June 21, 1546

I was very ill
when I woke up
this morning
but I went to
the Council
anyway

for I wanted
to advise
the Fathers
not to shun
the writing
of those
who oppose us

How else

I asked

can you know
what it is
they believe

And moreover

I added

knowing that
God guides the Church
you should be able
to show them
where they err

June 28, 1546

Today I leave Trent
for Padua

Paul has given me
permission to do so
to recuperate

If my doctor could
see inside my heart

he would discern
it does not palpitate
from weariness

Rather it is anxious
at the way the talks
are going

Should they lead
to dogmas that do
not parallel what I am
thinking

it will be my duty
to accept them
as from the lips
of Almighty God

And I will

Of that
there is no doubt

And I also know
at that moment
my heart will do
what I ask of it
and cease trying
to place an apple
into a cavity
fashioned for
an egg

February 2, 1547

I have just written
Edward the new king
that the persecution
of his father had been
as a ploughshare
that turned me
into a soil fertile
for the growth
of the godly seeds
of faith and hope
and charity

How strange it is
that in this world
a piece of parchment
is free to travel
where a man cannot

February 27, 1547*

I am three times grieved
at Vittoria's death

As a friend
she shared my vision
of the Church reformed

As a second mother
since my own was
martyred

she has given me
the strength to go on
when I felt I could not

As a poet
she has taught me
to see the world
in ways I had not

As with Contarini
so with her:

Another light has
gone out on the earth
but it now helps illuminate
our eternal resting place

November 11, 1549

Only when the wind blows
do we become aware
of the cords
that hold our tent
in place

Then we are grateful
they are there

In the same way
Paul was quietly
but firmly leading
Church reform

And he did so
even though some
within the Curia
saw change as threat
and some monarchs
felt a weaker Papacy
would give them
greater strength

Now Paul has gone
and I grieve for him
as I still do
for Contarini
and Vittoria

December 31, 1549*

This year I might have
become the first pope
from England

One more vote would
have created me
Paul's successor
but just as water
cannot flow uphill
so those cardinals
from Italy and France
could not bring themselves
to give me their support

When it became known
I was within one vote
of St. Peter's chair

the cardinals from the Empire
proposed to proclaim me
Paul's successor

I thanked them
for their support
but told them
I would not enter
the Vatican
by climbing
through a window

Even though I felt
there was no hope

I did go so far
as to decide
that if elected
I would be known
as the first George

the name
of my mother's father
whom Edward condemned
over 20 years
before my birth

August 7, 1553*

My body may never return
to the city of Venice

a city that rises
out of the sea

But 20 years of exile
have built the city
inside me

Perhaps the memory
I shall most cherish
is that of the glass-
blower's face:

the one whose studio stands
near San Salvatore

How humble he looked
when with his breath
he shaped a gracious goblet
from a gather of glass

Whenever I watched him
I felt I was present
in the Garden of Eden
as God breathed life
into Adam and Eve

November 20, 1554

As my ship sailed
out of Calais

I recalled stories
of pilgrims who died
in the sere of Sahara

Oases would shimmer
a few feet before them
and never come closer

But Dover's white cliffs
come ever nearer
so I who am thirsty
for England won't
suffer their fate

Nor will my parched countrymen
for I carry the cup of salvation
so long denied them

November 21, 1554*

When people ask how I felt
at the reversal of my attainder

I relate this allegory:

Once upon a time there was a king
who wished to set his wife aside
to marry his mistress

When the king asked one of his cousins
to help him achieve this objective

the cousin refused and reproached
his sovereign in very strong language

In a fit of rage the king commanded
the yeoman of the guard to toss
his cousin into the palace pigsty
with the other unfortunates
who had provoked their monarch's ire

For 20 years he was forced to live
among the swine but at the king's death
his successor signed an order for his release

A thousand baths have not removed
the stench from his nostrils

And more sadly still he knew there were many
who believed he would always stink

November 30, 1554

On this St. Andrews Day
anno domini 1554
at exactly 6:00 p.m.
I Reginald Cardinal Pole
stepped from the darkness
of London into Whitehall
alive with torchlight

As agreed upon two days before
the procedure was as follows:

First the Lord Chancellor
Bishop Gardiner read
on Parliament's behalf
a petition requesting
England be absolved
of heresy

With tears of joy
runnelling his cheeks
he then presented the Scroll
to Their Majesties

Together they held out
the document to me

And acting as legate
from the Vicar of Christ
on Earth

I then absolved
my island home
of heresy
in nomine Patri
et Filii
et Spiritui Sancti

Amen

December 24, 1555*

At the end
of our audience
Mary recalled
the first time
I met Philip and her
11 months ago
to the very day

How joyous I was
for I had just felt
a child leaping
in my womb

she continued

and we fell down
on our knees
in thankfulness:

Philip
you
and I

I then told her Majesty
that that evening
and everyone thereafter
I had prayed she might
be delivered of a baby boy

Then with eyes
brimful of tears
she said not bearing
the child had left her
with a sadness
deeper than
the deepest spot
in the Ocean Sea
Columbus would have
sailed across
60 years before

March 22, 1556*

Having heard
that Cranmer recanted
people are now asking
why we sent him
to the stake

They do not yet know
he reembraced his heresy
just an hour before burning

Nor did Mary and I ever believe
anything other than a fear
of fire had prompted
all six of his recantations

He would have had to die
even if he had not renounced
his recanting

for as a blind man
he led thousands
and thousands
of his countrymen
to the gates of hell

For that alone
he needed to die
many many times

Deep inside my heart
I admit his death
brought much sorrow

Those who might
not believe
what I am writing
need only recall
how few deaths
I assented to
when I governed
the Patrimonium
Petri

March 23, 1556*

Fear and denial knock
and the door flies open

So Peter found
at Gethsemane

But Jesus opens the door
to courage and assurance

So Peter found
after the Resurrection

becoming the rock
on which Christ built
His Church

This morning
when I was ordained
I felt the hand of Peter
on my head

filling me
with more certainty
and courage
than I have ever
known before

May I prove
ever worthy
of these gifts

March 24, 1556**

While my horse rested
at Lambeth Inn this morning

I watched a youth brush
an iron nail across a lodestone
over 30 times

When he dangled the nail
on a piece of string

it too sought the North

If only Cranmer could have seen
the nail take unto itself
the lodestone's power

he might have been able
to believe that bread and wine
become the very flesh and blood
of Jesus Christ

March 25, 1556*

I think of Canterbury
as a patient
Dr. Cranmer diagnosed
as being very ill
and for whom
he then prescribed
an amalgam
of many poisons

And intoxicated
by his heresy
he could not see
that what had not been ill
he was slowly killing

He will write
no more prescriptions
and it may take a while
but my regimen will bring
the English patient
back to health

Since we could discern
no difference
between the doctor
and his medicine

we consigned both
to the flames

Still though
I am sad
we had to do so

If Mary knew
of my sadness

she would chide me
heartily

December 22, 1556

Today the Queen dined
with me at Lambeth
and then after dinner
left for Greenwich
where she will spend
a lonely Christmas

As she struggles
to restore the faith
to England

she needs to have
a husband at her side

When Paul suggested
I do what I could to bring about
the marriage of Philip and Mary

I did so but I was not
then convinced
nor am I now
he was the man
she should have married

I later learned
the Emperor delayed
my return to England
for several reasons
after Mary came
to the throne:

one being he was worried
Mary might ask me
to marry her
instead of His son Philip

As a cardinal deacon
I could have been
dispensed

However Charles need not
have worried

for nothing was further
from my mind

February 27, 1557*

On my twelfth birthday
I remember coming upon
a dead lamb in the pasture
behind the palace

Three ravens were feasting
on its carcass

In disgust I tried
to shoo them away
but they kept coming
back and back
until only bones were
left

In somewhat
the same way
Paul will not let go
of his suspicion
I am a heretic

It is true
I have criticized
Holy Mother Church
from time to time
but only to keep it
worthy of its founder

Did He not
as Cardinal Caraffa
serve with me
on the Consilium

I know He carries
the weight of the Church
on His shoulders
in a perilous time

I know He does not
want the Church weakened
in any way

But to be accused
of heresy
by one I have
so much admired

Where my heart was
is now a lump of lead

October 24, 1558*

In one month
it will be four years
since I first met Mary
with Philip at her side

In all the years
I've known her
it was the only time
I ever saw her
broadly smile

Let us first discuss
affairs of state

I recall
she said to me

You are to be
the instrument
of bringing back
the Papacy
to England

But now to something
more personal

she said

Cardinal,
I have just felt
a child leaping
in my womb

a child
who will love me

a child
who will succeed me

Now she lies
very ill
and childless

And I am ill
with quartan fever
and the knowledge
Paul has summoned me
to Rome:

a summons Mary will not allow
to be delivered
and one which she will not let me
honour

November 3, 1558*

Over 250 heretics have died
in Mary's reign

How history will assess
the number of heretics
we have burned
is not for me to ponder

The question we must
answer is:

How would God have judged us
if we had not acted
to preserve the faith

It is however
with unquiet hearts
we find some heretics
remain heretical
despite our teaching
and our prayers

for we are aware
of what awaits them
in the hereafter
after Smithfield

November 10, 1558**

If people may be thought of
as cloaks to keep out the cold

I must admit I am about
to freeze

The first cloak to be taken off
was that of my cousin Henry
whom I deeply loved
when I was a child

The death of Contarini removed
one of the warmest cloaks
I have ever worn

Vittoria's was also comforting
and with her death
I have not felt quite warm enough
again

The doctors say
Mary will soon die
and when she does
I shall be left
without her cloak
to protect me
from the icy winds
that blow on me
from Geneva
and from Rome

November 17, 1558*

Mary died today
at dawnlight

I expect
to follow her
by twilight

for I feel a death-angel
fluttering around my body

In my will
I ask Elizabeth
to let me lie
in the Chapel
of St. Thomas
a Becket

Though she is
Anne's daughter

I feel confident
she will honor
my request

I remember
Vittoria once wrote
she felt at her death
her soul would
be given wings
to help it reach
its eternal resting place

Sinner though I am
I approach my death
with her assurance

Note on the Pole text

The absence of an asterisk after a date means the entry is factual. The presence of one asterisk * after a date means there is a factual element in the entry. The presence of two asterisks ** means the entry has been created to help portray an aspect of the Cardinal Archbishop's character.

Significant Events in the Life of Thomas Cranmer

1489 Born at Aslockton
1511 BA (Cambridge)
1514 MA (Cambridge)
1521 BD (Cambridge)
1526 DD (Cambridge)
1532 Married niece of Osiander, a Lutheran (second marriage)
1533 Consecrated Archbishop of Canterbury
1533 May 23, rendered judgment Henry and Catherine's marriage null
1533 May 25, rendered judgment Henry and Anne's marriage lawful
1534 April 17, wrote to Henry on behalf of Bishop Fisher and Thomas More, who were accused of treason
1534 In November, Parliament enacted law making Henry head of Church of England; Cranmer, Henry and Anne soon excommunicated
1536 May 16, visited Anne in Tower
1536 May 17, Henry and Anne divorced
1536 May 19, Anne beheaded
1538 October 15, served as godfather to future Edward VI; Mary, the future queen, was godmother
1538 Abandoned doctrine of transubstantiation but not the Real Presence
1541 November 1, handed note to Henry informing him of Queen Katherine Howard's improprieties
1546 Adopted a view of the Eucharist close to Z.H. Bullinger's formulation known as "symbolic parallelism"
1547 January 27, Henry died
1547 February 7, reappointed Archbishop of Canterbury
1547 In November, first real attempt by Parliament and Convocation to overthrow the orthodox religion and transform England into a protestant state
1547 November 5, approval given for marriage of priests and statutes for burning heretics abolished
1549 June 1, *First Prayer-Book of Edward VI* used in church
1553 July 7, Edward died
1553 July 19, Mary proclaimed Queen

1553 September 14, Cranmer sent to the Tower

1553 November 13, convicted of high treason and sentenced to traitor's death by hanging, drawing and quartering

1554 March 12, taken to Bocardo prison in Oxford with Bishops Latimer and Ridley

1554 In the fall, Mary acknowledged papal supremacy and restored statutes for burning heretics unless they recanted

1555 September 12-13, heresy trial for Cranmer held in Oxford

1555 October 16, Latimer and Ridley burned at the stake

1556 January 28, Cranmer wrote first of six recantations

1556 February 16, he was degraded at ceremony in Oxford

1556 Between February 13-17, papal legate Reginald Pole and Mary decided to burn Cranmer though he had recanted

1556 March 21, at age 67 Cranmer was burned at the stake

Significant Events in the Life of Cardinal Pole

1500 Born the son of Sir Henry Pole, a cousin of Henry VII; his mother Margaret Countess of Salisbury was a Plantagenet and first cousin once removed of Henry VIII

1515 Awarded an Oxford BA

1521 Completed further studies at Oxford and then went to Padua

1527 Returned to England and made Dean of Exeter

1529 Went to study at Paris where at Henry's request he acted as emissary to the faculty of theology during its debate on the validity of Henry's marriage to Catherine

1530 (a) July 2, Paris faculty of theology decided Julius II (1503-1513) could not issue a dispensation for the marriage of a widow (Catherine) with the brother (Henry) of her deceased husband (Arthur)
(b) November 29, Cardinal Wolsey died on his way to the Tower
(c) Pole declined Henry's offer of Archbishopric of York

1532 Went to Italy and did not return for over 20 years

1534 Bishop Fisher arrested for refusing to take the Oath of the Act of Succession acknowledging Henry VIII as head of the English Church

1534/1535 Became known to men who wished to reform the Church from within: e.g., Contarini and Ghiberti

1535 (a) June 22, Bishop Fisher executed
(b) Sir Thomas More beheaded for refusing to take the Oath of the Act of Succession
(c) Drawn to Venice by Bishop Caraffa, later Paul IV
(d) Contarini requested a reform commission be set up

1536 (a) January 2, Catherine died at age 50
(b) Pole wrote Henry denouncing his behaviour
(c) Invited to serve on a special reform commission along with Caraffa, Cortese, Contarini and others
(d) December 22, created Cardinal along with 109 others

1537 (a) January 22, Pole attainted by English Parliament
(b) In February the reform commission completed

Consilium de emendanda ecclesium
(c) Made papal legate by Paul III and sent on mission to try to persuade Catholic monarchs to ally themselves against Henry; mission unsuccessful

1538 August 29, younger brother Geoffrey under torture gave evidence that Henry chose to interpret as treason on part of their brother Henry, their mother and their cousin Exeter

1541 (a) In June his mother brutally executed
(b) In August Pole appointed governor of the Patrimonium Petri, whose principal city was Viterbo
(c) Pole and Contarini thought for a brief time the reunion of Christendom might be possible

1542 August 27, Pole's close friend Contarini died

1545 February 22, Pole appointed one of three Cardinals to preside at Council of Trent

1546 June 28, Pole left Trent for Padua to recuperate

1547 (a) January 27, Henry VIII died and Edward VI ascended throne
(b) February 27, Vittoria Colonna died

1549 December 10, Paul III died; Pole among candidates to succeed him

1550 (a) February 7, Cardinal Del Monte became Julius III
(b) February 17, Julis III appointed Pole to sit on a tribunal to deal with the protection of the faith
(c) In June, Pole relieved of governorship of Patrimonium Petri

1553 (a) July 7, Edward died and within 10 days Mary became queen
(b) Julius III appointed Pole papal legate to England

1554 (a) November 12, English Parliament's first order of business was to reverse Pole's attainder
(b) November 19, Pole set foot on English territory
(c) November 20, Pole arrived in Dover
(d) November 21, Pole arrived at Canterbury
(e) November 24, Pole arrived at Whitehall
(f) November 30, Pole absolved England of heresy
(g) December 24, Pole issued a decree saying no holder of church property would be liable for ecclesiastical

censure then or afterward

1555 May 23, Cardinal Caraffa elected Pope as Paul IV; he fought a war with Philip over Naples. He also started to move against the *spirituali*, of which Pole had been a member along with Contarini and others; Paul IV [as Caraffa] had been a member of the *zelanti*, a group in favour of a different approach to church reform

1556 (a) March 21, Cranmer burned at stake

(b) March 23, Pole ordained priest

(c) March 26, Pole consecrated Archbishop of Canterbury

1557 (a) In April, Paul IV withdrew nuncios and legates from Philip's kingdoms and deprived Pole of his legatine power; he also summoned Pole to go to Rome and appear before the Roman Inquisition to answer questions about the activities of the *spirituali*, many of whom were now dead; Mary kept summons from Pole and would not allow him to leave England

1558 (a) November 17, Mary died at 7:30 a.m.

(b) Pole died in the early evening on the same day as Mary

Sources for Canmer

• Ayris, Paul & David Selwyn (Eds.). (1993). *Thomas Cranmer: Churchman and Scholar*. Woodbridge, Suffolk: The Boydell Press.

• Belloc, Hilaire. (1931). *Cranmer*. Philadelphia: J.B. Lippincott Company.

• Gloucester, Edgar (Ed.). (1913). *The First and Second Prayer- Books of Edward VI*. (1549 and 1552). London: J.M. Dent & Sons, Ltd.

• Hutchinson, F.E. (1961). *Cranmer and the English Reformation*. London: The English Universities Press.

• MacCulloch, Diarmid. (1996). *Thomas Cranmer: A Life*. New Haven: Yale University Press.

• Pollard, A.F. (1905). *Thomas Cranmer and the English Reformation.* Rpt. 1965. London: Frank Cass & Co., Ltd.

• Ridley, Jasper. (1962). *Thomas Cranmer*. Oxford: The Clarendon Press.

• Suffield, G.E. (Ed.). (1964). *The Work of Thomas Cranmer* (Vol. 2). Appleby, Berkshire: The Sutton Courtenay Press.

Sources for Pole

• Fenlon, Dermot. (1972). *Heresy and Obedience in Tridentine Italy: Cardinal Pole and the Reformation.* London: Cambridge University Press.

• Loades, D.M. (1979). *The Reign of Mary Tudor: Politics, Government and Religion in England, 1553-1558.* London: Ernest Benn Limited.

• MacFarlane, K.B. (1924). *Cardinal Pole.* (The Stanhope Essay Prize). Oxford: Basil Blackwell.

• Schenk, W. (1950). *Reginald Pole: Cardinal of England.* Toronto: Longmans, Green and Co.

A Selection of Our Titles in Print

A Lad from Brantford (David Adams Richards) essays	0-921411-25-1	11.95
All the Other Phil Thompsons Are Dead (Thompson) poetry	1-896647-05-7	12.95
A View from the Bucket (Jean Redekopp) memoir, history	0-921411-52-9	14.95
bagne, or, Criteria for Heaven (rob mclennan) poetry	1-896647-32-4	15.88
Bathory (Moynan King) drama	1-896647-36-7	14.95
Best in Life (Ted Mouradian) self-help, business	0-921411-55-3	18.69
Beyond Borders (Laurence Hutchman) poetry	1-896647-25-1	13.95
CHSR Poetry Slam (Andrew Titus, ed.) poetry	1-896647-06-5	10.95
Combustible Light (Matt Santateresa) poetry	0-921411-97-9	12.95
Cover Makes a Set (Joe Blades) poetry	0-919957-60-9	8.95
Cranmer and Pole—Archbishops (Robert Hawkes) poetry	1-896647-33-2	15.88
Crossroads Cant (Grace, Seabrook, Shafiq, Shin) poetry	0-921411-48-0	13.95
Dark Seasons (Georg Trakl; Robin Skelton, trans.) poetry	0-921411-22-7	10.95
Dividing the Fire (Robert B. Richards) poetry	1-896647-15-4	4.95
Elemental Mind (K.V. Skene) poetry	1-896647-16-2	10.95
for a cappuccino on Bloor (kath macLean) poetry	0-921411-74-X	13.95
Gift of Screws (Robin Hannah) poetry	0-921411-56-1	12.95
Heart-Beat of Healing (Denise DeMoura) poetry	1-896647-27-8	4.95
Heaven of Small Moments (Allan Cooper) poetry	0-921411-79-0	12.95
Herbarium of Souls (Vladimir Tasic) short fiction	0-921411-72-3	14.95
I Hope It Don't Rain Tonight (Phillip Igloliorti) poetry	0-921411-57-X	11.95
Imprints and Casualties (Anne Burke, editor) lit. criticism	1-896647-24-3	19.63
Like Minds (Shannon Friesen) short fiction	0-921411-81-2	14.95
Manitoba highway map (rob mclennan) poetry	0-921411-89-8	13.95
Memories of Sandy Point, St. George's Bay, Newfoundland (Phyllis Pieroway) memoir, history	0-921411-33-2	14.95
New Power (Christine Lowther) poetry	0-921411-94-4	11.95
Notes on drowning (rob mclennan) poetry	0-921411-75-8	13.95
Open 24 Hours (Anne Burke, D.C. Reid, Brenda Niskala Joe Blades, rob mclennan) poetry	0-921411-64-2	13.95
Open Road West (Joe Blades) poetry	1-896647-30-8	13.95
Railway Station (karl wendt) poetry	0-921411-82-0	11.95
Reader Be Thou Also Ready (Robert James) novel	1-896647-26-X	18.69
Rum River (Raymond Fraser) short fiction	0-921411-61-8	16.95
Seeing the World with One Eye (Edward Gates) poetry	0-921411-69-3	12.95
ShadowyTechnicians: New Ottawa Poets (mclennan, ed.)	0-921411-71-5	16.95
Song of the Vulgar Starling (Eric Miller) poetry	0-921411-93-6	14.95
Speaking Through Jagged Rock (Connie Fife) poetry	0-921411-99-5	12.95
Tales for an Urban Sky (Alice Major) poetry	1-896647-11-1	13.95
The Curse of Gutenberg (Dan Daniels) short fiction	1-896647-23-5	16.95
The Longest Winter (Julie Doiron, Ian Roy) photos & fiction	0-921411-95-2	18.69
Túnel de proa verde / Tunnel of the Green Prow (Nela Rio; Hugh Hazelton, translator) poetry	0-921411-80-4	13.95
Wharves and Breakwaters of Yarmouth County, Nova Scotia (Sarah Petite) art, travel	1-896647-13-8	17.95
What Morning Illuminates (Suzanne Hancock) poetry	1-896647-18-9	4.95
What Was Always Hers (Uma Parameswaran) fiction	1-896647-12-X	17.95

www.brokenjaw.com hosts our catalogue, author events news, submissions guidelines, maunscript award competitions, tradebook sales representation, distribution and order fulfilment information. BJP eBooks of some titles are also available. Directly from us, all individual orders must be prepaid. All Canadian orders must add 7% GST/HST (Canada Customs and Revenue Agency Number: 12489 7943 RT0001).

BROKEN JAW PRESS, Box 596 Stn A, Fredericton NB E3B 5A6, Canada.